AF439943

Kerry of Kilfinan

AGAINST THE STREAM

A history of a Highland parish

Jamie Stewart Jones

CPHRC
editorial services

Kerry of Kilfinan: Against the Stream
History of a Highland Parish

CPHRC Editorial Services
506 Strathmartine Road
Dundee DD39BR
Scotland

First published in 1991.
The chapter on the powder mill was rewritten in 2021.

ISBN:

AGAINST THE STREAM

Acknowledgements

I WOULD LIKE TO RECORD MY GRATITUDE TO THE FOLLOWING people, not only for their encouragement and assistance in the preparation of this work, but also for their patience. They are, in no particular order:

Donald and Carol Sinclair for their inspiration, hospitality and friendship. Alistair Durie, Dr Anne Crowther and the secretaries of the Economic History Department at Glasgow University. Michael Moss and the staff at Glasgow University Archives. The History Department staff at the Mitchell Library in Glasgow. Murdo Macdonald, Argyll and Bute District Archivist whose assistance and hospitality went above and beyond the call of duty. Kennedy McConnell for his information about the powdermill. Robin Watson of Ardlamont House, who put me in touch with Mrs E. Shaw of Tignabruaich. The staff at the Scottish Records Office and New Register House in Edinburgh. Julian Agnew, Mairi Darroch, Simon McFarlane, Bryce Mowbray, Simon and Karen Fraser, Mairi McIntyre and Mairi D's parents.

Last, but by no means least, I would like to give a special thanks to Linda Gourlay, whose friendship and support over the past months has kept me going.

To one and all, thanks! The mistakes are, of course, all my own.

Jamie Stewart Jones
Glasgow
October 1991

Contents

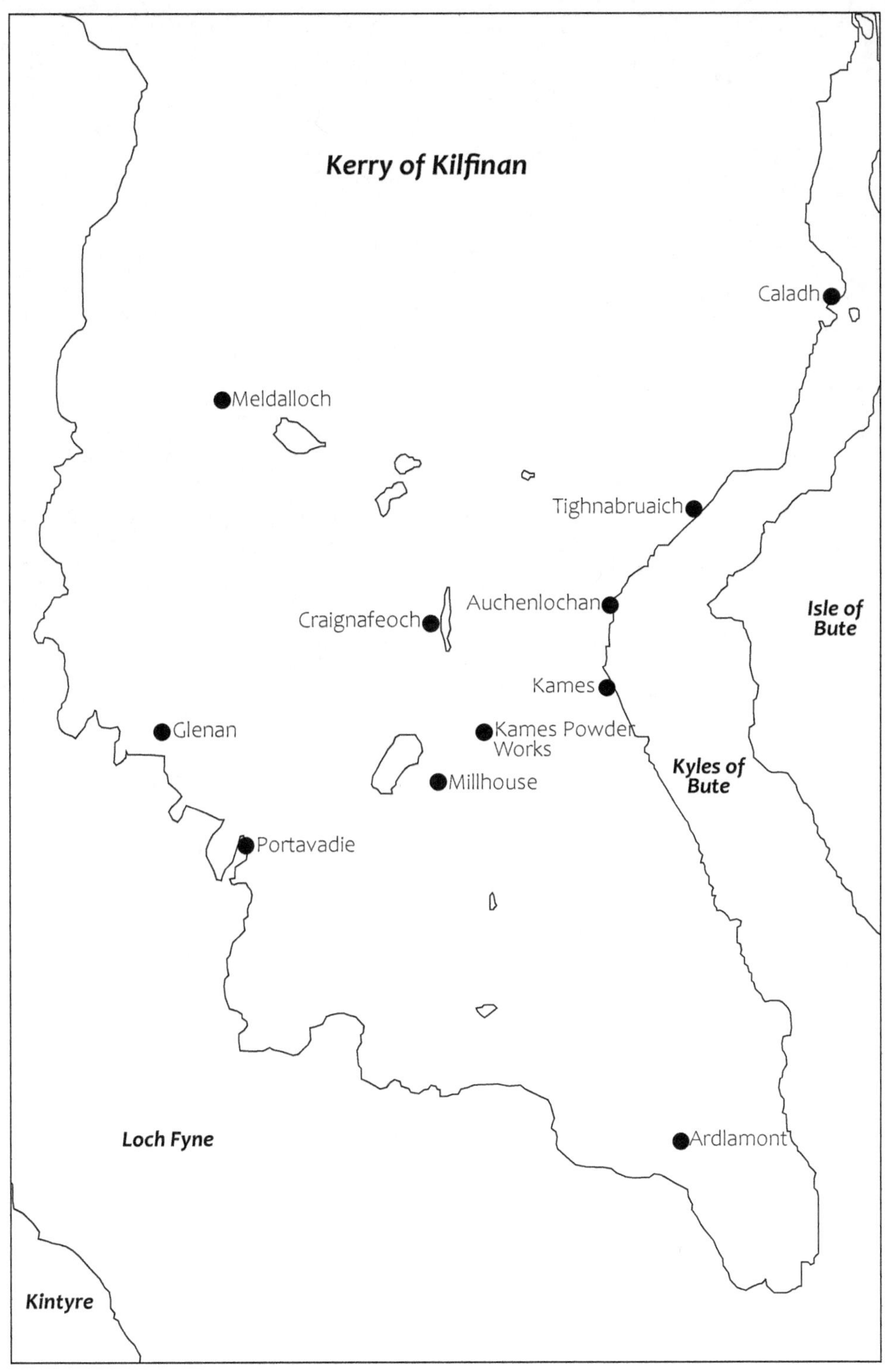

Map of Kerry of Kilfinan showing approximate locations.

Introduction

Never forget that only dead fish swim with the stream
MALCOLM MUGGERIDGE

THE HISTORY OF THE SCOTTISH HIGHLANDS DURING THE 19TH century is a subject of some fascination and much controversy for many. The pathetic plight of the Highlander, whose traditional lifestyle had become anachronistic, has been the object of many a romance, as academics, lay historians and novelists alike have sought to find explanations, excuses or myths to explain and describe their fate. Inevitably, in the more formal descriptions, and perhaps due to the grandeur and magnificence of the landscape, this has led to the emergence of two main camps, which are perhaps best described as the *realists* and the *romantics*.

The *realists* seek to explain the story of the Highlands by examining the economic realities affecting the region and its inhabitants. They tend to describe a rapidly growing population that was increasingly unable to support itself. The relative poverty that afflicted most of the people and the recurrence of famine stretched whatever little traditional support systems existed far beyond their breaking point, resulting in the need for intervention by landowners, governments and charities. The remoteness of much of the Highland region from the rest of the United Kingddom tended to mitigate against any form of industrial developments on a scale large enough to soak up the excess population and inject capital into the area, while landowners were more concerned with their desires to make their land pay, all of which combined to make it seem to those in power that large-scale land clearances and forced emigration to make space for sheep was the only *realistic* option for those in power.

The *romantics* tend to take a different, although not necessarily opposing point of view. Many are less insistent about the inevitability of the events as they unfolded, while arguing more could have been done to prevent the worst excesses of the clearances and eventual depopulation of the glens and mountains. They argue that for many years capital flowed from the periphery to the cities of Edinburgh and London as Highland landlords neglected and rack-rented their tenants to finance their urban lifestyles and that it was they who were largely responsible for the breakdown of the traditional Highland way of life and the region's poverty.

While both viewpoints have their worth, it is a fundamental truth that most of the history written about the Highland experience has tended to be of a more general and overarching nature, often resulting in assertions of events in one part being presented as a fact of what happened across the region. Even in the few and relatively inaccessible local studies that have been produced, they tend to be specific to areas that will confirm what is said to be the general trend and are rarely heard above the noise of the plethora of publications about the Jacobite Rebellions and their aftermath.

This book examines the economic development of the southernmost quarter of the Highland Cowal parish of Kifinan – Kerry of Kilfinan – over the period 1790-1870, which has become known in the United Kingdom as the Industrial Revolution. This will enable us to discern the very real peculiarities of Kerry of Kilfinan during this period compared to the fates described for many other parts of the Scottish Highlands.

We begin with an examination of the changes in agriculture and land use. As was true in most of the Highlands, land use in Kerry underwent a significant transformation during the period of the late-18th and early-19th century known as the Industrial Revolution. During the early part of this period, traditional farming practices prevailed. People tended to live in small *fermtouns* (farm towns) of a few close-knit and often related families that cultivated small plots of land and kept a few animals for fleece, milk and meat. The residents of these *fermtouns* engaged in subsistence farming, often growing just enough to feed themselves and pay the rent to the landlord. In good years they might produce a small surplus that could be used for trade, but rarely enough to invest in improvements. However, the growing interest of landowners in new scientific agricultural techniques that involved the consolidation of land into larger parcels separated by hedges or walls began to reshape the landscape throughout the country.

The agricultural revolution, which had begun in England before moving north through the Scottish Lowlands, gradually made its way to the Highlands. Innovations such tree felling and stone clearance allowed fields to get much larger, while crop rotation, the use of fertilisers and improved drainage were implemented. These changes, which allowed the productivity of the land to increase, led to the displacement of the *fermtouns* and the dispossession of their occupants as the landowners drove ahead with their plans to create larger and more efficient farms operated by fewer people. This process, which became known as the Highland clearances, resulted in many people being evicted from their homes and thrown off their land to make way this new scientific method. Across much of the Highlands, where most of the land is unsuitable for arable farming, the people were displaced by sheep, which were more profitable.

In Kerry, the impact of the agricultural improvements was palpable and by the middle of the 19th century, large parts of the parish had been converted to pasture for sheep. The social fabric of the community was altered as families that had lived in the farmtouns working the land for generations were forced to leave. While some found paid employment on the newly created farms, many others left for the cities of the central belt or boarded ships bound for the

New World and the Antipodes, contributing to the depopulation of the Highlands.

The role of landowners in this transformation cannot be overstated. In Kerry, as elsewhere in the Highlands, the landlords and their factors wielded considerable power. With almost complete control over the fate of their largely deferential tenants to whom there was often a perceived bond of kinship, those who held legal title to the land would prioritise their economic gain over any idea of noblesse oblige or desire to maintain social stability. The shift from small-scale farming to large sheep farms was driven by the greed for higher profits and was fuelled by rising wool prices during the early part of the century. It is important to note that not all landowners were driven by the desire to increase their income at the expense of all else. Some – a very few – invested in improvements to their estates by building roads and schools and purchasing tools for their tenants in moves designed to improve the local population and invest in their own futures. However, such efforts were often overshadowed by the broader trend of depopulation and economic hardship. In Kerry, a few of the more socially progressive landowners sought to balance the desire for economic development with a sense of social responsibility. However, it is also fair to say that, in the global Highland context, they were the exception rather than the norm.

Kerry is bounded on three sides by water, which resulted in fishing, particularly fishing for herring on Loch Fyne and the Sound of Bute, playing an increasingly important role in the lives of the people and the economy of the parish during the first half of the 19th century. The herring boom, which peaked in the mid-century, brought both opportunities and challenges to the community. Herring was in high demand across the United Kingdom and in continental Europe, where it was a staple food. This demand drove a surge in fishing activity along the entire west coast of Scotland.

In Kerry, the herring industry provided an alternative source of income for many of the families that had been displaced by the changes to agriculture. The village of Kilfinan saw the development of new infrastructure to support the industry, including the construction of piers, curing sheds and warehouses. The economic impact of the herring industry on Kerry was significant. It brought a measure of prosperity to the area, with some families able to improve their living standards thanks to the income it provided. However, while the seasonal nature of herring fishing meant that it provided employment during the months when there was less agricultural work available, the industry was also precarious. Herring stocks often fluctuated dramatically from year to year, leading to periods of boom and bust.

This instability made it difficult for families to rely solely on fishing for their livelihood. Nevertheless, the herring industry brought a number of social changes to Kerry. The influx of seasonal workers from other parts of Scotland and Ireland created a more diverse population, and while this increased diversity could and often did result in tensions, it also brought new ideas and cultural influences. The presence of fishery companies and traders introduced a whole new world of economic dynamics, with some local entrepreneurs thriving while others struggled to compete.

One of the more unusual aspects of Kerry's economic development during the first part of the 19th century was the establishment of a gunpowder works on the moor between Glenan Woods on the shores of Loch Fyne in the west and the small settlement at Kames on the Kyles of Bute in the east. The choice of Kerry for this industry might seem surprising given its rural and relatively remote location. However, several factors made it an attractive site for gunpowder production. First, the availability of raw materials such as charcoal, sulphur and saltpetre was crucial. Kerry's woodlands provided a source of charcoal, while the importation of sulphur and saltpetre was facilitated by the parish's coastal location. The relative isolation of Kerry also made it a safer location for such a hazardous endeavour. Explosions were an ever-present risk in gunpowder production, and locating the works away from major population centres reduced the potential for catastrophic accidents.

The gunpowder works quickly became an important part of Kerry's economy, providing jobs for local residents and attracting skilled workers from outside. The industry required people with a wide range of skills, from manual labourers to chemists and engineers. This diversity of employment opportunities helped stabilise the local economy by offering alternative paid employment to that which was available on the land or in the herring boats.

The presence of the gunpowder works also had a multiplier effect on the local economy by stimulating demand for housing, food and other goods and services that benefitted local businesses. The works also contributed to improvements in the parish's infrastructure, with the construction of roads and quays and the development of transport links that facilitated the import of raw materials required in the manufacture of black powder and the export of finished explosives.

During the early 19th century, the parish experienced the birth of a service industry, albeit on a modest scale. Inns and taverns opened to cater to visitors, travellers and locals, while small shops opened to supply the new population of wage earners with the goods needed to meet their essential needs.

The growth of the fishing and gunpowder industries created a requirement for more sophisticated services, including financial services, transportation, law and medicine. As the local economy diversified, so too did the service sector. The presence of industries meant there was a demand for banking and insurance. Local entrepreneurs and investors needed access to credit and financial advice, which led to the establishment of banks and lending institutions. Similarly, the risks associated with fishing and gunpowder production created a market for insurance services.

By the mid-19th century, the service sector in Kerry had expanded and modernised. Improved transport links, including better roads and the advent of steamships, facilitated trade and communication. This connectivity allowed local businesses to reach wider markets and access goods and services from other parts of Scotland and beyond.

Education also became a priority, with the establishment of schools and training facilities. An educated workforce was essential for the continued growth of the service sector, and efforts were made to improve literacy and vocational skills among the population. These educational initiatives were often supported by progressive landowners and philanthropic organisations.

Tourism emerged as a significant component of Kerry's service sector, driven by the natural beauty of the region and the romantic allure of the Highlands. The late 19th century saw the beginnings of tourism in Kerry, as visitors from other parts of the United Kingdom and beyond were drawn to the scenic landscapes and the Highland life that had been romanticised by writers such as Sir Walter Scott and Robert Louis Stevenson. The construction of railways and the expansion of steamship services opened up access to the Highlands, Kilfinan included.

Tourism brought new economic opportunities to the area. Inns and hotels were established to cater to visitors while local guides offered tours of the picturesque countryside. The tourism industry provided employment and stimulated demand for local crafts and produce, contributing to economic diversification. The impact of tourism on Kerry's economy was profound. It created a demand for services ranging from accommodation and dining to entertainment and retail. In turn, this led to further investment in infrastructure and services, creating a virtuous cycle of growth and development. However, tourism also brought challenges. The influx of visitors could strain local resources and disrupt traditional ways of life. There was a growing need to balance the economic benefits with the preservation of Kerry's natural and cultural heritage. This balancing act required careful planning and management to ensure tourism could be sustained without compromising the character of the area.

As the century progressed, the popularity of tourism and the increasingly easy access to Cowal from the industrial and commercial heartland of the west central belt's towns and cities was responsible for the emergence of a new development. The newly wealthy urban middle class that had emerged in the industrial towns of west Scotland during the Industrial Revolution – the industrialists, entrepreneurs, importers, exporters, lawyers and doctors – started purchasing parcels of land on the eastern shore of the parish, where they set about erecting large stone villas in which they and their families would spend time away from the dirt and noise of the cities. This development opened up new opportunities and challenges for the residents of the parish and for its economy.

It is important to recognise, however, that not everyone benefited from these developments. The elderly, disabled, the poorly-educated and the unemployed often found themselves marginalised alongside those who still spoke Gaelic. Traditional support systems, such as the extended family networks and communal assistance that was once found in the *fermtouns*, were strained by the social and economic upheavals of the period. For the elderly and disabled, the transition from a subsistence economy to a more market-oriented one could be particularly challenging. Many of these older residents had spent their lives working in the *fermtouns* or on the herring boats, and the shift to larger agricultural enterprises or industrial employment left them without viable livelihoods. Similarly, disabled individuals, who might have found ways to contribute to traditional *fermtoun* economies, faced greater barriers in the new economic environment.

In response to these challenges, a range of charitable and governmental initiatives emerged. Local charities, often supported by wealthier residents and landowners, provided some assistance to the most vulnerable. Almshouses and poor relief funds offered limited support, but these measures were often insufficient to meet the needs of the growing number of disadvantaged residents. Government intervention also played a role, particularly during the latter part of the century. The Poor Law Amendment Act of 1845 extended the poor relief system to Scotland, providing a framework for more systematic support. However, the implementation of these measures varied, and many residents continued to struggle with poverty and deprivation.

While it would be wrong to criticise either the *realist* or *romantic* schools, it is hoped that this small contribution can provide a contrast with the general trends that may illuminate the fact that not every Highland parish suffered the same fate and that perhaps more did indeed 'swim against the stream'. The history of Kerry of Kilfinan during the 19th century offers a nuanced perspective on the broader trends that have attracted the interest of many historians of the Scottish Highlands. While the parish did indeed experience many of the challenges described by both realist and romantic historians, it also demonstrated resilience and adaptability. The diversification of the economy, the development of new industries and the growth of the service sector all contributed to a more complex and varied economic landscape.

If it does little else, this contribution highlights the importance of examining local histories in helping us obtain a fuller understanding of the past. By focusing on Kerry of Kilfinan's specific experiences, we can better appreciate how general trends played out in many different ways across the Highlands. This approach allows us to appreciate the richness, diversity and complexity of the Highlands and its history, moving beyond simplistic dichotomies to embrace a more comprehensive view of the region and its past.

Agriculture and Land Use

*All that is solid melts into air… and men at last are
forced to face with sober senses the real conditions of
their lives and their relations with their fellow men*
KARL MARX

IT IS CERTAINLY TRUE TO SAY THAT THE KILFINAN OF 1790 WAS
substantially unaltered from that which had existed in 1690, at least
as far as the mode of cultivation employed was concerned. The parish
minister, Alexander Macfarlane, in his *Statistical Account of 1793*,
was driven to remark that the tenants were so 'much attached to
the ancient mode of cultivation, that modern improvements… can
scarcely be said to have found their way to our latitude' (Macfarlane 1793: 237).

In 1802, Kerry, the southern part of Kilfinan parish, was
divided into 24 *fermtouns* (ABDA 1802 Valuation Roll), each of
which could be home to anything up to 15 families (Macfarlane 1793:
242). With the records available, it is impossible to be certain about
the average duration of leases; however, Macfarlane does indicate
that some of them were 'pretty long' (1793: 242), though there is
more modern evidence that implies the standard 19-year lease was
not very common in Kilfinan (McKechnie 1938: 316; Macfarlane
1793: 368). This can be substantiated by the fact that the Rev. Joseph

Stark claimed, in 1843, that seven and nine-year leases were the norm (1843: 368).

Within Kerry there were no villages, although at Meldalloch to the north there was a mill, and at Mecknock (later known as Millhouse) in the centre, there was a mill and a blacksmith. The land itself, thus divided and leased, was cultivated following the run-rig pattern common to pre-improvement agriculture, with the main crops being oats, potatoes, barley and peas (Macfarlane 1793: 243), all of which gave yields of between three and six times that sown, except for potato, the yield of which exceeded 20 times that planted (Macfarlane 1793: Smith 1813: 327).

There was an experiment carried out at Ardlamont in the early 1790s to ascertain whether wheat could be grown. However, there is no evidence to suggest this cash crop was taken up by the poorer farmers who, it would appear, tended to stick with what they knew (Macfarlane 1793: 238; Stark 1843: 367).

In addition to the crops, most of the tenants also kept cattle housed in a byre all year round, with the manure being collected, mixed with soil, and used as fertiliser. The only beasts that were allowed to graze on open pasture were those kept for their dairy produce (Macfarlane 1793: 238; Stark 1843: 367).

The largest landowner in Kerry during this early period was John Lamont of Lamont (landlord from 1767-1816), whose estate stretched to include most of Kilfinan and substantial parts of the neighbouring parishes of Glendaruel, Kirkmichael and Inverchoalin.

Lamont much preferred the social life of Georgian Edinburgh to that of his Highland estate, which he generally left to his factor to run and manage. However, he had to finance his expensive lifestyle, and it soon became apparent to him that his expenditure far exceeded his income. As a way of increasing his revenue, Lamont appeared keen to follow the example of many of his peers, and in 1790 he introduced the black-faced sheep to his farm at Inveryne (McKechnie 1941: 316). This was followed in 1772 by the granting of a 12-year lease for four Kerry farms to a Fletcher Dunans of Glendaruel (McKechnie 1941: 317), although it is impossible to say without doubt that this was for a sheepwalk. What it is possible to say, however, is that Lamont's introduction of sheep on to his estate centred more on Inverchoalin parish where, by 1813, there were 583 sheep per square mile compared to 85 in Kilfinan.

To place these figures into some context, it is perhaps worth mentioning that the average number of sheep per square mile in Argyll and Cowal, respectively, was 120 and 277 (Smith 1813: 325). Similarly, there is some evidence to suggest that, despite the amalgamation of several farms by 1793, the traditional *fermtoun*, utilising traditional methods, was still very much the norm (Macfarlane 1793: 242). Indeed, by 1802 there appears only to be two amalgamated leases in the whole of Kerry – Acadachewn, Corrachow and Blair's Ferry; and Innins and Rowanbank – and of these, only the former belonged to Lamont (ABDA 1802 Valuation Roll).

It would appear Lamont quickly abandoned the idea of placing Kerry under sheep in favour of awarding longer leases to single tenants, perhaps in the hope these tenants would improve the land, thus allowing him to raise rents over a period of time (Macfarlane 1793: 242). To finance his lifestyle in the meantime, he embarked upon a course that involved selling off and mortgaging large tracts of his inheritance (McKechnie 1941: 336).

Upon his father's death in 1816, General John Lamont of Lamont became the new master of the estate. Very early on, the General intimated that he intended to reverse his father's policy of single tenancies by subdividing 'a great part of the farms of Auchagoyle, Achadalvorie… and others [back] into crofts' (McKechnie 1941: 348).

His reasons for this decision are unclear, although there did exist at that time a school of thought, of which he was probably aware, that believed estate clearance was a short-sighted policy and that it would be better for everyone if landowners were to encourage crofting. Not only would this ensure that the land would be cultivated, allowing the rents to be raised gradually to 'arrive at a greater height' (Smith 1813: 278) than they would otherwise, but also, according to their argument, it would create the conditions 'necessary for the encouragement of population; without which no country can prosper... for without an abundance of labourers no important improvement can ever be effected' (Smith 1813: 35). It is possible, if not probable, that the fact Kilfinan's population had declined by 21% during the last half of the 18th century (a period when the overall Highland population was expanding at a rate 40% greater than the Scottish average [Mitchison 1981: 4]) made the General more receptive to such suggestions (Smith 1813: 325). And, of course, there is also the possibility that he wished to provide land for men returning from the French Wars to be considered, although how many such men there were is far from clear.

When General Lamont inherited the estate from his father it was much reduced in size, strictly entailed and burdened with fairly large debts (McKechnie 1941: 348–9). The General, however, managed to reschedule the estate's debts in 1818, which enabled him to reduce the rents – which had risen rapidly under his father's stewardship – by 25 % (McKechnie 1941: 348–9).

This undoubtedly provided a fillip for the tradional farmers of Kerry, and there appears to have been little pressure exerted upon them to change their ways and adopt more modern methods. It would not be stretching the truth to say that by the time of the General's death in 1829 life carried on much as it always had – subsistence agriculture supplemented by herring fishing.

Things were set to change, however, with the arrival of the steamship in the early 19th century. The changes were gradual at first, but with an assuredness that was to gather momentum until the traditional way of life had been well and truly extinguished.

The arrival of the steamers finally wrested Kerry from the remote Highlands and placed it securely within the orbit of the central Lowlands, within easy reach of the major industrial centres of the Clyde coast. There is evidence that some of the landowners were beginning to make real improvements to their lands by introducing drainage, enclosure and the granting of 19-year leases to single tenants (Stark 1843: 309–10).

Further evidence of the growing interest in improvement is the fact that in May 1848, Archibald James Lamont of Lamont obtained a loan of £1,390, paid in four instalments of £351, £526, £109 and £104, from the Enclosure Commissioners of England and Wales, to enable him to begin providing drainage to his lands at Ardlamont (ABDA Register of Sasines 1846–50).

A further advance of £1,610 was obtained in November 1852 to enable him to complete the work (ABDA Register of Sasines 1851–55). Inevitably, such improvements were to have a profound effect on the way of life in Kerry.

In total, between 1841 and 1871, the number of people in Kerry describing themselves as farmers had fallen from 34 to 19, at least six of whom farmed more than 100 acres by the later date. Further, while 148 people stated they were mainly employed in agriculture in 1841, this had fallen to 72 by 1871.

Smout and Wood (1990: 95) claim women formed an important part of the agricultural labour force, performing tasks as diverse as running the dairy and gathering harvests. This being so, it is perhaps important to note that the census returns during this time rarely included the occupations of the women who lived in the communities – and this is particularly true of the 1841 census. It is therefore probable that by excluding female occupations, the census returns underestimated the total numbers employed in agriculture.

In any event, it appears as if the agricultural revolution had arrived in Kerry – albeit belatedly. Even so, by the 1870s there were still at least six farmers and their families scratching out a living with less than 10 arable acres each.

However, it is clear that the trend was away from such small holdings, and it could be that these smallholders were simply working out the remainder of their leases at the end of which their lands would be reparcelled into larger units (NRH Census 1841; 1871). Regardless of the many improvements in land use in Kerry during the 19th century, it nonetheless remained dominantly pastoral, with only around 8% of the land available being cultivated (Groome 1885: 363).

At the beginning of our period, Kerry contained several fairly evenly distributed small communities, or *fermtouns*, of roughly equal population. The inhabitants of these communities were mainly peasant farmers with short leases cultivating using traditional methods.

The small size of the holdings and the relatively high rents (particularly before 1816) more or less ensured an economic return below or at subsistence level.

Due to the location of the parish, however, they could and did supplement their income and diet by fishing for herring on Loch Fyne during the summer – a habit Macfarlane believed to be an obstacle to agricultural improvement in the 1790s (1793: 240).

By 1870 the situation had altered radically. Apart from the farm at Colacha, a community of three crofts, and some other isolated crofts, most of the farms had expanded and come under single tenancy, while others, like Glenan, had been completely abandoned. Paradoxically, over this same period of agricultural improvement, Kerry's population more than doubled, to reach 2,038 by 1871 (NRH Census 1871).

To discover the reasons for this expansion and the obvious absorption of the displaced population, we must explore other aspects of Kerry's economic history.

Fishing

What is required is a leap of faith
SOREN KIERKEGAARD

IT HAS BEEN STATED ABOVE THAT THE INHABITANTS OF KERRY regularly engaged in herring fishing on Loch Fyne. Initially, fishing was merely a supplementary means of income to their main pursuit of small-scale farming. However, as the century progressed, fishing was to become one of the most important economic activities of the parish, eventually supplanting agriculture, especially in terms of the numbers employed.

In 1793 there were 21 fishing boats in Kilfinan, each employing four men. How many of these boats were operated by men residing in Kerry is impossible to calculate, however. Most of the fishing was carried out on Loch Fyne, although the boats did occasionally venture as far as Loch Long and the Ayrshire coast in pursuit of the herring shoals.

It was evidently a quite remunerative occupation, with full-time fishermen – those who fished the entire season – earning as much as £10 to £24 per annum. Such men, however, were in the minority. Most of the fishing was carried out by farmers and agricultural labourers who, because of their commitments to the land, could only engage themselves for part of the year. Consequently, their earnings from this occupation were very much less: indeed, as Macfarlane puts it, they were 'very inconsiderable' (1793: 246).

There is also some evidence to suggest that a number of the men of the parish engaged themselves to work on the large bounty vessels that were encouraged by government legislation dating from the 1750s in an effort to break the Dutch stranglehold on the herring industry (Gray 1978: 5). Owing to the time such vessels were at sea, it is most probable that the men who worked on them were the sons of farmers who were of more use to the family leaving home to earn a wage that could supplement the household's income.

What is clear, though, is that at the end of their engagement these men generally returned to the area to find local employment wherever they could.

It is difficult to determine just when fishing ceased to be a secondary occupation in Kerry. However, the industry was given a significant boost with the relaxation of the Salt Laws in 1796 (Gray 1978: 6). While it may be fair to say that there would have been greater employment opportunities with the expansion of the industry that followed this relaxation, it is unlikely the people of Kerry would have been able to capitalise to any great extent.

Before fishing could become a primary occupation in Kerry, its own fleet would have to expand dramatically, and in order for it to be able to do that certain conditions would have to have been met. One of the major constraints on the development of the industry in Kerry was the nature of land holding then common.

The subsistence level at which the majority of the population existed meant the capital necessary to build boats and purchase nets simply did not exist, and there is no evidence of any support for the industry from any of the landowners.

In any case, the conservatism of the local population, which has been alluded to above, would tend to suggest that the desire to move from agriculture to fishing simply did not exist, and that the population was quite content to maintain fishing as a secondary occupation (Macfarlane 1793: 241).

By the 1830s, however, the situation had changed. The steamship, which was by that time a common sight on the waters around Kerry, opened up a new market for Loch Fyne herring. For the first time, herring could be landed at the Broomielaw in Glasgow just a few hours after it had been caught.

In addition, there was also push pressure introduced by the improvements in agriculture mentioned above, which resulted in the displacement of large numbers of people.

While there are no figures available to tell us just how many people actually moved into full-time fishing, it is not inconceivable that many of them, seeing which way the winds of change were blowing, made such arrangements for themselves or their children.

So it was that by 1840 there were 68 boats operating out of bays around Kerry, employing a total of 204 men (at least 103 of whom lived in Kerry [NRH Census 1841]) and 91 ancillary workers such as gutters, packers, repackers, cleaners, dryers and coopers. Kerry also got its first fish curer in 1838 (SRO Private Statistical Book AF26/26).

While the curer bought the fish off the boats, there is no evidence to suggest that he either engaged certain boats for the season, agreeing to purchase their entire catch for a set price, or that he actually had a financial stake in any of the boats – a practice that was common on the east coast of Scotland. Loch Fyne curers did, however, guarantee a minimum price for fish, thus preventing price collapse (Gray 1978: 122).

Most of the herring caught in Loch Fyne was landed at Inveraray, where it was sold and loaded onto the Glasgow-bound steamers, some for export by rail to Billingsgate in London.

While in 1809, before the arrival of the steamers, the total catch of cured herring recorded at Inveraray was 65 barrels (SRO AF26/1), by 1840 a total of 5,796 barrels of cured herring passed through the town (SRO 26/29). One can add to this total the numbers that passed through other Loch Fyne-side towns, such as Lochgilphead, where 1,549 barrels were landed in 1832 (SRO 26/24), giving us some idea of just how much this industry had expanded.

Traditionally, Loch Fyne fishermen used the drift net method. This involved using nets that were 24 feet deep and anything up to 1,350 yards in length. Because of the size and weight of the net, large boats costing anything from £60 to £100 and crewed by between four and six men were required. The boats were sailed into the middle of the loch, where their nets were put out over the stern at sunset. Once the nets were out, the boats simply drifted with the wind, tide and currents until dawn, when they were hauled back into the boat – a slow and laborious task. This method of fishing was much preferred by most of the regular fishermen since the initial capital outlay restricted the number of people who could afford to get involved, while the mesh size ensured only mature fish could be caught, thereby preserving stocks. Both of these factors combined to ensure the price of herring remained relatively stable (SRO AF37/142).

During the first half of the 19th century, much of the population displaced as a result of changes in proprietorial policies converted to fishing. However, for many of them, drift netting was simply out of the question: they could not afford the large boats and nets. The only solution was the cheaper trawling method, which involved the use of seine nets of up to 170 yards in length and 14 yards in depth, and which cost as little as £4 10s. The only other requirement was a small rowing boat costing no more than £20. Trawlers would cast their net in a large circle and then haul it in, trapping everything within it. As there was no need to wait for the fish to enmesh themselves, the net could be recast several times, enabling trawlers to catch entire shoals of mature and young herring in a single day (SRO AF37/142).

Inevitably, there was no love lost between the trawlermen and the drift net fishermen, with the latter seeing their livelihoods come under increasing threat. The government eventually stepped in and passed legislation outlawing trawling for herring. The initial Act, passed in 1850, proved ineffective as it was widely ignored, especially in Tarbert, where it was reported that 'a number of drift boats [are] in… but are getting very few herrings – the drift net fishermen are looking at the trawlers landing boatloads' (SRO AF37/2). In 1859 a new Act was passed outlawing trawling, and a gunboat, the *HMS Jackdaw*, was dispatched to patrol Loch Fyne.

However, it was clear that the trawlermen, who mainly came from Tarbert, had the support of many, including the powerful Duke of Argyll, who told the captain of the *Jackdaw* that 'rigorous enforcement of the Act against trawling… where much capital has been invested in illegal equipment, is not desirable' (SRO AF37/2). In December 1859, the following circular from the Deputy Comptroller of Coast Guard was issued:

> I have to acquaint you that their lordships have informed me that it appears to be desirable that for the moment, the strict observance of the restrictions with respect to trawl nets should not be enforced. You will, therefore, give direction (confidentially) to this effect to the respective officers of Coast Guard under your command (SRO AF37/16).

Largely as a result of uncontrolled trawling, catches of herring dramatically increased. In 1862, while the *Jackdaw* was playing cat and mouse with the trawlers, 582 boats landed a record 62,295 barrels (SRO AF26/14). In 1867 Loch Fyne was officially opened to trawling, and by 1870 there were 528 boats fishing the loch (SRO AF26/39), including more than 100 trawlers (Gray 1978: 121).

Although there is little empirical evidence to suggest that any Kerry fishermen were involved in trawling, Gray's claims that trawling was confined to the south of Otter Point, and that fishing had become a primary occupation in the lower parts of Loch Fyne, with 'land ceasing to be an interest' (Gray 1978: 121-3), combined with the sheer extent of illegal trawling, and the large start-up costs involved in drift netting (£200 compared to £25 for trawlers in 1864) does tend to suggest that some Kerry men could have been involved at one time or another. It is doubtful if the trawlermen aspired to drift netting as the financial returns were much lower (Gray 1978: 122).

It is probable, then, that following the legalisation of trawling in 1867, the full-time fishermen would tend to convert to trawling, while drift netting may have been reserved for those who still had some interest in the land.

Such was the success of the fishing industry in becoming a primary occupation for many in Kerry that by 1869 its fishing fleet had grown to number 81 skiffs and smacks registered in Rothesay (SRO AF7/113) and described as operating from the Kyles of Bute, with an indeterminate number operating from Loch Fyne-side bays between Ardlamont Point and Auchalick.

In total, by 1871, 126 Kerry men gave their occupation as fishermen (NRH Census 1871), substantially outnumbering the numbers employed in agriculture, and there is also evidence suggesting some pupils were taken out of school periodically to assist in the industry (ABDA CO6/5/172/1).

While the main fishery in Kerry was herring, many fishermen used the closed season (January to May) to fish with baited hooks and lines. Most of this type of fishing was carried out in Loch Riddon.

There does not appear to be any record of any full-time line fishermen: perhaps the herring was too valuable and abundant a prize to be ignored. Another form of fishing that existed on a very small scale was bag net salmon fishing in the Kyles of Bute (Stark 1843: 368). However, only one family, by the name of Scoular – probably relatives of Arthur Scoular of Innins – can be identified as being involved in this pursuit (NRH Census 1851; 1861).

Similarly, there are occasional reports of poaching for freshwater fish in the inland lochs and lochans. However, due to the illegal nature of this pursuit, there are no figures available that could allow us to determine just how widespread this activity was.

The Powder Mill

But the nature of things is such that nobody in this world ever gets anything for nothing. These amazing and admirable advances have to be paid for
ALDOUS HUXLEY

DURING THE EARLY PART OF THE 19TH CENTURY, THE LOCAL LAND-owners were struggling to make any money out of their largely marginal properties, placing pressure on the communities that lived there as they sought to introduce agricultural improvements. In the late 1830s, two businessmen approached Archibald James Lamont of Lamont and pitched him an idea that was to transform Kerry of Kilfinan.

The two businessmen were Thomas Gray Buchanan of Glasgow and John Macallum, who had been born at Auchrossan Farm in 1800. What they wanted from Lamont was a lease for the moorland that stretched between Auchgoyle Farm and Millhouse and for some land at the shore at Kames, upon which they proposed to erect buildings and construct a steamer quay. A deal was struck, and in 1839 the Kames Gunpowder Company began production.

The powder mill was set up in Kerry for a number of reasons, the main ones being its remoteness, the availability of cheap unskilled labour, a reliable water supply, low rents and its ready access to the sea from where raw materials and finished goods could be transported. The fact that Macallum was a native of the parish, with the local knowledge that implies, will also certainly have figured in the decision.

While negotiations over the mill were being conducted, the road trustees debated where best to build a quay and how best to link it with the main road from Kilfinan to Ardlamont. The main protagonist in this debate seems to have been Lamont, who in 1838 took out an interdict preventing the road trustees from building on his land. However, in 1839, once the establishment of the powder mill was certain, Lamont completed what became known as the *Black Road* himself, providing the missing link from Kames Farm to the shore. As a result, the trustees confirmed their decision of July 1832 to build a stone quay at Kames, which Lamont insisted be available to his tenants. The powder mill set about building a quay of its own, the *Black Quay*, to load and unload saltpetre and the finished gunpowder and the buildings required for storing and processing the raw material.

The land on which the mill was constructed was little more than moor and thus of little agricultural value. There is also no record of the initial duration of the lease agreed between the company and Lamont. Nevertheless, the mill quickly established itself as a producer of quality powder, which led its owners to purchase feudal possession of the land in 1850, with the property purchased including an 'area occupied by reservoirs on the lands of Craignafeoch', thereby ensuring a ready supply of water to power the machinery.

Given the volatile nature of the product and the need for regular tests of the explosive, it was important for it to be relatively remote. However, this did not negate the essential requirement for a labour force, transportation links and an abundant source of power. Kerry met all these requirements. It had a widely dispersed population and a ready workforce attracted to the idea of a regular wage. It had proven steamer links with the industrial heartland of Scotland and a fairly good connection between the mill and the quay, which was improved with the construction of the new road in 1857, almost half of which was paid for by the mill. Finally, by utilising Craignafioch

Burn, it had access to the waters of Asgog Loch and, later, to the reservoir constructed just to the south of Meldalloch Loch.

Not only was the gunpowder mill the largest single industry in Kerry, employing 142 people in 1861 and more than 200 by 1870, but it was also by this latter date the largest gunpowder mill in the whole of Scotland and was largely responsible for the relatively large-scale migration of industrial workers and their families to the area. A substantial minority of those who described themselves as powder workers in 1861 were from England: there were also mechanics, engine smiths and coopers from the Glasgow area. However, migration notwithstanding, the great majority of mill employees were natives of Kilfinan who worked a 57-hour week for regular pay that allowed them to loosen their traditional attachment to the land, thereby enabling the landowners greater scope in their land improvement policies.

A further consequence of the mill's establishment was an element of internal migration from the traditional centre of the parish, Kilfinan, to Kerry. Perhaps this migration was merely an augmentation of many other factors that contributed to Kerry becoming the most populated part of the parish by 1851. For the first time, Kilfinan had at least two recognisable villages where goods and services could be obtained: Millhouse and Kames, which in 1841 had a combined population of 221, rising to 697 by 1871.

While for most of its lifetime the mill was able to produce high-quality powder without much incident, there were occasions when disaster struck – often fatal, sometimes catastrophic and always appalling. It was the nature of the business in the days when safety was rarely a consideration and when people worked very long hours in dreadful conditions, often while hungry, tired and without breaks.

Tragedy was no stranger to the mill at Kames. The first recorded fatal accident was in 1842 when two men were killed in an explosion. On 5 August 1846, the powder in the corning house, where the powder was sieved, suddenly exploded, killing seven men, whose 'mutilated remains were found scattered at a great distance', with the explosion being heard as far away as Inveraray.

Three years later, the powder mill's steamer, the appropriately named *Guy Fawkes*, struck the Paddle Steamer *Marquis of Stafford* near Gourock, resulting in the death of Archibald Maclachlan, a crewman on the *Guy Fawkes*.

More tragedy struck on 20 April 1854 when two men were killed in an explosion in the mixing room, with the added tragedy that it was but 'a few years since a similar explosion took place here when the father of the person who was killed outright on this occasion was blown to pieces'.

More fatal accidents happened: on New Year's Day 1857 four men died in an explosion, then on 25 May 1858 five men and one boy lost their lives. On 3 December 1863 the corning house was struck by lightning, causing it and several other buildings to explode, costing the lives of seven men. It is said this explosion was heard in Rothesay and Dunoon.

The greatest tragedy at the mill, however, took place on the morning of Friday 11 March 1870 when the half ton of powder stored in the wooden press house exploded, shattering the building to pieces, destroying two neighbouring grinding mills and igniting the powder inside them, killing four men and a 14-year-old boy who was standing outside the door to the press house loading tubs onto a cart to be transported to the *Black Quay*.

The bodies of the four men – Alex McGlashan, John Carswell, Duncan McPherson and Hugh Stewart – the boy – George Smith – and the cart horse were blown to some distance and their limbs scattered far and wide. The driver of the cart had a miraculous escape, as he had left the cart to run an errand elsewhere in the works, only returning to his post after the explosion. Contemporary newspaper reports describe the discovery and condition of the bodies in visceral detail, explaining the difficulty faced in identifying the remains.

The explosion was described as being so powerful that 20-inch square beams and rocks were sent careering through the air for hundreds of yards, with one projectile landing in a field next to a ploughman, creating a six-inch deep furrow that extended for a length of 20 feet. Houses for miles around were shaken and damaged and the explosion was heard in Rothesay, to where the West Highland mail steamer, the *Pioneer*, was dispatched with all haste to offer help.

However, this was not the end of the matter. In a rather unexpected development in August 1870, Duncan Macullich, procurator fiscal for Argyllshire, prosecuted the mill's owner, John Macallum, and manager, William Sealy, for storing 455lb more powder than legally permitted in the press house. The court found the defendants guilty and fined them £20 each with £3 7s. 6d. costs and declared the excess gunpowder forfeit. The defendants immediately appealed, with the case appearing before the High Court of Justiciary in Edinburgh on 31 October 1870, where the Lord Justice General, the Justice Clerk and Lords Cowan, Dens, Ardmillan, Neaves and Jerviswood upheld the ruling of the lower court.

While the mill continued manufacturing gunpowder during the First World War, falling demand led its new owners, the Nobel Gunpowder Company, to close it down in 1921. However, in a ghastly final twist of fate, John McGilp, who was dismantling machinery in the mill, was killed when a spark from his hammer ignited powder that had accumulated under the floor.

In 1926, a fish curing company from Aberdeen was so impressed by the success of the herring fishing on nearby Loch Fyne that it purchased the former saltpetre works on the shore at Kames with the intention of establishing a curing station there. Unfortunately, little is known of this project, which may perhaps reveal yet another part of the history of Argyll's secret coast.

And what about the remains of the mill today? Well, while a lot of the site is now overgrown, its physical mark on the countryside is there for all to see.

From the *Black Road* linking Kames to the heart of the parish at Kilfinan and the road that continues along the shore, past the shinty field and on towards Caladh, past the piers that brought the wealthy tourists and homeowners to this northern shore of the Kyles of Bute. The mill owner's lodge, saltpetre stores and the *Black Quay* are still there and used for other purposes. In the hollow across the road from the Mill Cottages, many of which are now available as holiday lets, one can find the remains of many of the buildings in which the saltpetre was turned into black powder, there you can also see what is left of the tramlines along which the product was moved through the mill as it completed its journey on the manufacturing process. One can also see the channel along which water flowed from the Craignafeoch Burn to power the machinery and in which men cowered for their lives during the occasional explosions.

The most instantly recognisable remnant and a reminder of the significance of the tragic and fortunate legacy of this important site is perhaps not the road, the quay or the roofless and overgrown remains of buildings and tramways, but the more prosaic symbols of the mill 'clock', known as the *Dolphin Bell*, which stands at the entrance to Millhouse Cemetery, the small rusted mortar that was used to test the power of the explosives and, most poignant of all, the plaque containing the names of all those whose lives were cut short while working at the mill.

The Newcomers

You will comfort me with… the sight of the little children carrying the golf clubs of your tourists as a preparation for the life to come
GEORGE BERNARD SHAW

BEFORE THE ADVENT OF THE MOTOR CAR, THE LOCHS AND RIVERS of Scotland's west coast were not considered obstacles to be surmounted: rather, these expanses of water were the lifeblood of the communities bordering them, providing the links across which large amounts of goods and people could be transported efficiently and economically. It was the land that was the obstacle. As a result of this dependence on waterborne transport, most of the communities on the west coast had ferries linking one with the other. In this respect, Kerry was no exception.

In 1793 Kilfinan had three ferries: one from Otter across Loch Fyne to Kilmichael, another 'across Lochfine on the line of road from Rothesay, in Bute, to Tarbert' (Macfarlane 1793: 248) and a third across the Kyles of Bute from Blair's Ferry. These three routes linked the Highlands with the Lowlands, and contributed to Rothesay's role as the main market town for the surrounding parts of Argyll.

While by the 1820s these ferries were still relatively important, they were rapidly becoming anachronistic remnants of a bygone age – an age when the communities on Loch Fyne formed a closed and largely self-sustaining economy. Developments both beyond and within these communities during the early 19th century, however, forced them to the realisation that the world had moved on.

The arrival of the steamer was merely an outward expression of that reality. Kerry, along with countless other similar communities had to adapt or die. Kerry, as we have seen, adapted, and by 1843 it was reported that 'since the introduction of steamboats… travelling by the ferries has entirely ceased' (Stark 1843: 369).

By the mid-1830s, steamers were a regular sight off the coast of Kerry. The fish that were caught on Loch Fyne were taken by steamer to Glasgow. The steamer brought the saltpetre from South America to Kames and then took the finished gunpowder to its destination. However, as well as carrying goods, the steamers also carried people. While Highlanders and their goods could now reach the Lowlands in less than a day, the reverse was also true: Lowlanders could now reach the Highlands.

By 1856, anyone with 1s. 6d. and time to spare could embark on a four-hour journey from the Broomielaw to Kames and Tighnabruaich on such boats as the *Mail* and the *Sir Colin Campbell*, encountering 'scenery [that]… cannot fail to impress upon the mind of every beholder the rugged beauty and sublimity of our Scottish lochs' (*Glasgow Herald* 19 May 1856). The introduction of modern tourism to this part of Scotland was to have a profound affect on Kerry, one that was to be even more significant that that of the gunpowder mill.

The construction of Tighnabruaich pier during the 1840s or 1850s by Arthur Scoular of Innins,[1] whose small estate included

---

[1] The first definite mention of Tighnabruaich pier is in the valuation roll for 1858–9, which clearly states Arthur Scoular of Innins was the proprietor. However, there are

the farms of Over Innins, Rhuban and Caladh, allowed him to grasp the opportunity offered by the arrival of tourists, and in 1853 he began feuing off parts of his lands on the shore between Innins Wharf and Rhuban Burn (ABDA Valuation Rolls 1802; 1858-59; Abbreviated Register of Sasines 1851–55).

What began as a trickle quickly grew into a deluge as plot after plot was sold off and the new village of Tighnabruaich was born. By the end of 1859 a total of 19 properties, most owner-occupied, had been build on feus from Scoular, including Tighna-craig House (later renamed Craigengower), which was owned by Adam Black MP, the publisher of the *Encyclopaedia Britannica* and of the novels of Sir Walter Scott (ABDA Valuation Roll 1858–59; Dictionary of National Biography Vol VI, 1855). Between 1841 and 1871, Tighnabruaich's population had increased by more than 760%, to number 398 by the later date, with the greatest expansion taking place after the mid-1850s (NRH Census 1841; 1851; 1861; 1871).

In 1853, John Malcolm of Poltalloch, who owned a small amount of land between Kames and Auchinlochan farms, gave notice to the road trustees that he intended to build a road on his property between the properties owned by Lamont and Scoular, thereby completing the link between Scoular's detached shore road and Kames (ABDA CO6/2/2/4).

He followed up the trustees' approval of his plan by purchasing the superiorities of Middle Innins and Auchinlochan farms from Alexander Stewart in June 1854 (ABDA Abbreviated Register of Sasines 1856–60 / 659). In December 1859, eight months after his new road had been completed, uniting his lands with the piers at Kames and Tighnabruaich, Poltalloch began selling feus (ABDA Abbreviated Register of Sasines 1856-60; ABDA CO6/2/2/4). This consummate piece of business led to the emer-

---

several more ambiguous references to a landing point on Unin's land, some dating as early as 1846.

gence of a fourth village, Auchenlochan, which by 1871 had a population of 70-80 (NRB Census 1871).

While his neighbours were capitalising on Kerry's very good fortune, Lamont was facing serious financial problems – so serious that in 1862 he was forced to mortgage his entire Ardlamont estate to various parties for £10,900 (ABDA Abbreviated Register of Sasines 1861–66). In 1856, Lamont had placed an advert in the *Glasgow Herald*, offering the sale of 'very beautiful feus… on the Lamont estate to any extent that suits offerers' (16 April 1856). In an attempt to attract potential purchasers, in 1855 he had 'resolved on extending the new stone pier about 40 feet, by the erection of a wooden jetty that would allow the steamers… in at all states of the tide' (ABDA AGN 418–57; *North British Daily Mail* 24 September 1855).

However, the location of the pier and the land to be feud was ill chosen. While Poltalloch and Scoular were able to offer unspoiled land, all Lamont had to offer was – as we have seen – the site of the gunpowder mill's saltpetre refinery and quay. Potential feuars were simply not interested in purchasing land in such close proximity to a factory: after all, that is precisely what they were hoping to escape.

Duncan Colville's journal of his weekend in Tighnabruaich in June 1857 offers an insight into the attractions Kerry had to offer wealthy Victorians:

> 14 June 1857. Taynabruich is beautifully situated… on the Kyles of Bute. Behind the house hills and woods, on either hand coast, before Bute… As we come out of church, some man of great enthusiasm is pouring forth as I have never seen any man do. His flock are seated on the hillsides… I was much struck with the sight. It reminded me of the Conventicles… Delightful walk to boat – then sail home. The salt water so very pretty… The gentlemen of the party retired to a pleasant spot where they (i.e. we) bathed. How delightful the first few strokes! But lo how cold! Having dined… we soon remembered we had proposed climbing a high hill

behind – which we did… the view worthy of twice the climb. All moor land behind extending in fine sloped hills. In front, beyond the sea, Bute, and yonder Arran's rocky slopes (ABDA CO6/1/13/9).

The charms of the wide open spaces, glorious vistas and cold water that appealed to Colville were merely a taster. For many Victorians, the Highlands were a place for more active pursuits, such as fishing and hunting. Shooting was available on Poltalloch Moor, between Auchenlochan and Millhouse, while, due to the lack of any rivers, fresh water fishing was restricted to the several small burns and inland lochs. While most of the proprietors retained the shooting and fishing rights on their property, Poltalloch leased his out. His shootings were rented to the Lamont estate, while his fishings were leased to Campbell of Glendaruel (ABDA CO6/1/13/9). This tends to suggest that while Lamont and Scoular were attempting to retain their respective estates as agricultural concerns, Poltalloch was intent on developing his for tourists.

The construction of the many substantial Victorian villas in Tighnabruaich, and the smaller houses in Auchenlochan in such a short space of time required huge amounts of labour. The wealthy new residents required services, they needed clean water supplies, shops, a bank, a Post Office, their gardens needed tending and their food needed to be prepared and served. In their wake, the wealthy residents brought about numerous new employment opportunities for the people of Kerry and beyond. It is this to which we shall now turn.

The Services

*It was the ambition of my father and mother
that I should be a tradesman. They knew
what it was to live on a labourer's wage*
DAVIE KIRKWOOD

KERRY'S RELATIVELY REMOTE LOCATION DURING THE EARLIER period, and the poverty of most of its inhabitants, meant that most of the objects that were required for everyday use had to be manufactured and maintained within the community.

During the 1790s, Kilfinan as a whole had 36 weavers, 22 tailors, 11 shoemakers, three smiths, seven wrights, three millers and one flaxdresser (Macfarlane 1793: 253).[1] Of this total we can only be certain that the smiths and the millers were resident in Kerry.

It is possible that the weavers were supplied with wool from Lamont's sheep farm at Inveryne and that the woven cloth became his property to be sold.

Unfortunately, it is impossible to ascertain the quality of the cloth produced by the Kilfinan weavers, although it is probably fair to assume that it was not very high. Nor is it possible to locate them

---

[1] Macfarlane is careful to warn, however, that 'perhaps some of them, who work at times at different trades, may be twice reckoned'.

within the parish.[2] Similarly, we cannot be certain from where the tailors obtained their cloth or where they resided, although it is possible that, in order to keep costs down, they were mainly supplied from the Kilfinan weavers and that they lived close to them.

If this was indeed the case, then it would be fair to assume that their products were sold within Kilfinan, both to residents and to passing trade, rather than consciously exported.

However, there are no written records of such a system and, while it remains a possibility, we cannot make any more definite claims (Macfarlane 1793).

By the 1860s, the numbers involved in the textile trade in Kerry had declined to two weavers – one at Glenahuil and the other at nearby Achadachoun (NRH Census 1961). What type of cloth they made and where it was bound is unknown. It was, however, a dying trade.

As there were no real villages in Kerry during the early period, there was no real centre to the community. Most of the inhabitants had access to some land from which they could meet most of their basic needs, with any excess produce being sold at the market in return for money and services. In such a community, most of the small day-to-day services could be purchased through a system of barter, with money only being necessary for major transactions, the purchase of imported goods, transportation, rent, taxes and ale.

There had always been a restricted market for domestic servants in Kerry, particularly in the homes of the larger landowners and wealthier tenants. Although there are no figures available prior to 1841, it must be assumed that Ardlamont House had always employed a certain number of servants. By 1841, the young Archibald James Lamont, his wife, daughter, mother, sister, brother and a friend were tended to by a retinue of 15 servants and a gardener,

---

[2] In his account of 1843, Stark notes that 'the sheep reared in this part of the country are…in general of a small size, owing to the pasture on the hill not being of the best description' (Stark 1843: 368).

all of whom lived on the grounds (NRH Census 1841). A few other wealthy residents also employed servants to varying degrees.

The establishment of the gunpowder mill in 1839 resulted in the emergence of a small industrial labour force centred on the villages of Millhouse and Kames, whose needs had to be met by others in exchange for money. Consequently, a new service sector of merchants and craftsmen sprung up around them. By 1851, Millhouse and Kames had a collection of grocers, tailors and cobblers to keep the residents fed and clothed, and an innkeeper and spirit merchant to keep them happy (NRH Census 1851).

The arrival of tourists to Kerry also provided new opportunities in the service sector. By 1864, the Royal Hotel had been established on the shore at Auchenlochan, and here was another hotel at Tighnabruaich,[3] opposite the Post Office that had been established there in 1855 (ABDA AGN 418–57; North British Daily Mail 24 September 1855). By the end of our period, between them, Auchenlochan and Tighnabruaich had eight shops and the services of butchers, grocers, bakers, drapers, dressmakers, washerwomen, tailors, innkeepers and shoemakers: they even had an unemployed foxhunter. Further, Tighnabruaich had a sub-Post Office and a branch of the Royal Bank of Scotland (ABDA Valuation Roll 1869–70; NRH Census 1871).

In total, between 1841 and 1871, the number of people describing themselves as having occupations that can be classed as being in the service sector had risen from 37 to no fewer than 178, making it by far the largest sector of Kerry's economy.[4] Furthermore, most of the 178 lived in Tighnabruaich and Auchenlochan,

---

[3] Now called the Tighnabruaich Hotel.

[4] The service sector includes those who listed their occupation as domestic servants, general servants, housekeepers, cooks, shopkeepers, tailors, cobblers, drapers, dressmakers, washerwomen, governesses, bank clerks, post mistress, pier porter, gardener, doctors, nurses, messengers, excisemen, dealers and hawkers. Farm servants are not included.

while in 1841 most were employed at Ardlamont House (NRH Census 1841; 1871).

As well as being largely responsible for the expansion of Kerry's service sector, the wealthy new residents also precipitated a construction boom, particularly between 1850 and 1870. Before 1850 it had been traditional practice for the inhabitants of the parish to build their own houses. A typical 18th-century lease would require the tenants to secure stone for the walls and thatch for the roof, all of which would be provided by the landowner (McKechnie 1931: 306).

The tenants were also responsible for the construction and maintenance of the boundary walls on their property and, before the 1843 Argyll Roads Act, which introduced a compulsory road tax for which all inhabitants were liable (ABDA CO6/2/20/10), for the construction and maintenance of Kerry's roads through statute labour. This, combined with the fact there were only a handful of substantial properties in Kerry, such as Ardlamont House, the church and manse, and a few cottages and farmhouses belonging to the wealthier tenants, there was almost no need for resident crafts-men involved in construction.

The low level of mainly small-scale construction that was traditional in Kerry, and the limited demand for building trades-men did not alter until the arrival of the gunpowder mill. The large amount of building work involved in setting up the mill, including the processing houses, the workers' houses, the saltpetre refinery and the quay, was undertaken by a construction company from Glasgow (Stark 1843: 366). And although there would have been a number of labouring jobs that Kerry men could do, the limited amount of work, combined with the strict apprenticeship rules, would rule out their being trained as artisans.

The real boom in building work came about during the 1850s and 1860s, with the construction of the large Victorian villas and hotels that line the waterfront at Tighnabruaich. The virtual guar-antee of regular work for a long period of time meant many of the artisans who came to build these houses stayed on, moving from one job to another. By 1861, there were 35 artisans living in Kerry, including 15 stonemasons in Tighnabruaich alone, from as far afield as Roxburgh in the borders, Uist in the north and Anstruther in the east (NRH Census 1861).

It is unlikely, however, that many Kerry men would have been able to obtain apprenticeships. Rather, any who were looking for work would have been employed as unskilled labourers or as carters. By 1871, as the feus began drying up, the boom in house-building was coming to an end, with the result that the number of artisans had dwindled to around 20.

Poor, Paupers and the Unemployed

Gude-man, will ye giff me your charitie,
and I sall declair yow the black veritie
Sir David Lindsay

NO STUDY OF AN AREA'S ECONOMIC DEVELOPMENT WOULD BE complete if it ignored the effects of these changes on those who, for whatever reason, could not, or would not, participate in the economy.

Unemployment, or non-employment, in any of its guises is as important an economic factor as the development of new industries or changes in land use.

In Kerry, the chief responsibility for relief of the 'poor, aged and impotent' lay with the established church through the Kirk Session. The finances that allowed discharge of this duty at the beginning of our period were largely raised by traditional methods, such as 'collections made a church on Sundays, at marriages and baptisms, with small dues for proclamations, fornication fines and fees made for the mortcloth'.

The monies raised in this way were supplemented by 10s. interest from an unspecified sum that was donated to the poor in 1737, and there is also evidence that would suggest the heritors made regular voluntary donations, although whether or not they had agreed to a voluntary assessment is far from clear (Macfarlane 1793: 250; SRO CH2/880/1).

As we have seen, before the advent of the steamship, Kerry was unequivocally located in the Highlands. Its remoteness during the earlier period was an effective barrier to the creation of any alternative forms of employment to subsistence agriculture. As a direct consequence of this, the necessary conditions for the effective functioning of the Poor Law could not possibly be met, and even with the funds mentioned above Kilfinan simply did not have the economic wherewithal to properly fund the system. Consequently, during this early period, the 'principal support for the poor was begging' (Macfarlane 1793: 250).

If, through 'sickness or accidental misfortunes', any of the poor were prevented from begging, the parish treasurer would furnish them with 'such small donations as will be temporary relief' (Macfarlane 1793: 251n). To enable the authorities to distinguish between authorised beggars, vagrants and the able-bodied poor, the Kirk Sessions were instructed to 'make up… annually, lists of the poor within their parishes, and to provide them with badges, regularly numbered, with the name of the parish marked on them' (ABDA CO6/1/22/4). The Settlement Laws were to be strictly adhered to.

There is clear evidence that although the statute did allow parishes to distribute relief to all cases of poverty, regardless of cause, in Kerry only the impotent poor: that is, 'the old and infirm, the insane and destitute children' (Mitchison 1988: 251) who had no relatives or friends who could support them, were provided with relief from the church.

The able-bodied poor were denied both parish relief and the right to beg: if they could not find employment, they would starve. For many, one alternative to such a fate would have been emigration to the developing industrial towns and cities of the Central Belt. However, the operation of the Settlement Laws and the requirement for a letter of introduction ensured that even this avenue was fraught with difficulty. Another escape route was to join the armed services. A meeting of the Commissioners of Supply for Bute in 1778 considered a letter from the Secretary at War, Lord Barrington, which stated:

> It is the King's strict directions that no man shall on any account be pressed into the service who are not... able bodied, idle and disorderly persons who cannot, upon examination, prove themselves to exercise and industrially follow some lawful trade or employment or to have some substance sufficient for their support and maintenance (ABDA CO5/1/1).

From this it would appear that, at least during the French Wars, the government had a favoured method of dealing with the idle poor. In any event, there are no statistics that could enable us to assess just how much of a problem unemployment was in Kerry during this time.

It is not unreasonable to assume that the emergence of new sectors to Kerry's economy during the first half of the 19th century greatly reduced any unemployment problems that the area may have experienced. The increasing prominence of herring fishing as a primary occupation, the establishment of the gunpowder mill and the growth of tourism and its associated service industries all combined, as we have seen, to reverse what appeared to be Kerry's fate in the earlier decades: marginalisation and depopulation.

By 1843, the number of paupers had increased to 34; however, when measured against the growth in population, their overall proportion inthe community had declined from 2.8% in 1813 (Smith 1813: 325) to 1.8% in 1843 (Macfarlane 1793: 250, 253; Stark 1843: 366, 371).

However, these figures do not bring any light to the level of unemployment in Kerry, as they do not include the 'idle' poor. In 1843, Joseph Stark stated that 'it is chiefly to the aged who have no near relatives able to maintain them that such aid is given' (Stark 1843: 371). Smith's 1813 survey, though, suggests that Kilfinan suffered a level of pauperism that was higher than the average for the county of Argyll at that time (Smith 1813). Considering Kilfinan's almost unique development following that date, however, it would not be unreasonable to assume that by the end of our period its proportion of paupers declined much faster as the new employment opportunities in non-agricultural sectors meant individuals could be more readily supported by friends and families without resort to the Poor Law.

With the introduction of the new Poor Law in 1844, a compulsory assessment was levied on each parishioner. By 1849, Kilfinan's poor assessment was made via the roads assessment, at a rate of 8d. in the pound sterling (ABDA CO6/7/21/1). This infusion of money into the board's coffers enabled it to increase the benefits available to the poor, as well as allowing it to help more people. By August 1848, the board distributed £70 2s. 8d. to 53 paupers, £1 7s. to four occasional poor, paid £4 4s. to Dumbarton parish, thatched a pauper's cottage at a cost of 6s. 6d. and paid £1 8s. 6d. for three funerals. In addition, the board undertook to pay for the school fees of the children of paupers and to inquire into their progress (ABDA CO6/7/21/1).

A further development came in 1851 when, to take advantage of a government grant, the board appointed a parish medical officer. The board also decided to pay half of the poor relief in cash and half in meal, ensuring food was always available to paupers and their families.

By 1854, the parish doctor was receiving an annual salary of £40 from the public authorities in addition to the fees he charged his wealthier patients. The medical officer was charged with visiting all paupers four times per year, treating them where necessary, and for preventing the spread of epidemics. With the outbreak of cholera in the parish in September 1854, the medical officer was empowered to 'hire a horse when called to attend… and to procure the necessary medicines' (ABDA CO6/7/21/1).

In 1854, and after much debate, the board decided to establish a *reception house* for the poor in a vacant building at Meldalloch.

By 1861 this house had eight residents, including two children aged nine and six. The average age of the adults was 64 (NRH Census 1861). There seemed to be a great reluctance on the part of the board to call this establishment a poor house, although there is evidence that its residents were expected to perform some tasks in exchange for their relief.

A report from 1859 stated that the *reception house* was satisfactory and that 'it was gratifying to the board that not only were no complaints made by the inmates, but that they expressed themselves as being well cared for'. A later minute perhaps explains the absence of complaints:

> George Lamont, pauper at Meldalloch reception house… has complained about the inspector's conduct towards himself and other paupers… Lamont was called to the meeting where he stated his complaints. Three other paupers were called who refuted everything. Lamont was reprimanded and told he was a liar and behaving improperly. The inspector was given powers to send him to the district poorhouse if he misbehaves again (ABDA CO6/7/21/2).

Although the parochial board evidently had enough money to relieve the poor, it seems that their narrow definition of what constituted deserving poor remained largely unaltered across the 80 years of this study.

The minute books of both the Kirk Session and the parochial board give example after example of people who were excluded from relief for one reason or another. On the other hand, the board was not slow to threaten legal action against people whom it believed should take responsibility for some of the paupers. That said, however, around the mid-1840s there was a noticeable change of attitude towards many of the poor.

There was a definite move towards providing relief in the first instance, then asking questions later. Perhaps the best illustration of this is the case of the widows and orphans of Hugh Stewart and

Duncan Macpherson, both of whom lost their lives in an explosion in the gunpowder mill in March 1870. The board decided to grant the usual and necessary relief, 'reserving all claims the board may have against the mill for such advances as may be made' (ABDA CO6/7/21/2). Such actions would have been almost unimaginable prior to the 1840s.

We have seen that there was a general improvement in provision for the poor over the entire period. While in 1793, the Kirk Session merely awarded begging licences to the impotent poor, by 1870 paupers were being fed, they had access to free medical treatment and their children were being educated.

The position of the able-bodied poor, however, does not appear to have been addressed: they were left to the charity of friends and neighbours and had no claim on parochial funds. This unfortunate situation was largely a result of a legal dispute over the relief of unemployment in the Abbey parish of Paisley in 1821, following which 'the expression persons "not able to work for their living" applied to those who were disabled… rather than those whose employment was merely temporarily suspended', and the words "'poor, aged and impotent" are to be read as "aged poor and impotent poor"' (Mitchison 1988: 261).

However, it is probable that, at least in Kerry, the problem of unemployment was negligible. Throughout the 19th century, with the growth of the new industries, it can be assumed that there were greater employment opportunities and that whatever employment there was would tend to be limited in extent and frictional in nature.

Conclusion

IN HIS BOOK ABOUT THE ECONOMIC AND SOCIAL HISTORY OF EASTER Ross, Mowat quotes a writer who suggests that Easter Ross 'is a district which is "in but not of" the Highlands' (Mowat 1981: 139). The same can be said of Kilfinan, particularly after the arrival of the steamers during the early nineteenth century.

During the earlier period, Kerry of Kilfinan appeared to be embarked upon the same course as many other Highland areas. This is especially true when agricultural methods and land use are examined. At the beginning of our period, Kerry of Kilfinan's subsistence-level agriculture was typical of pre-improvement Scotland. This relative backwardness acted as an effective bar to any form of economic development as there was no surplus produce available to permit any significant part of the community to break out of its dependence on agriculture (Gershenkron 1962; Rostow 1959).

A further bar to economic development during the early period was the fact that the largest landowners, the Lamonts, suffered from the same failings as many of their peers. As we have seen, John Lamont was eager to play his part in Edinburgh life. His expensive habits placed a great strain on his estate's revenues and resulted in the removal of capital from Kilfinan.

His entailing of what was left of his estate may have protected it from attack by his creditors, but it also left his successors to foot his bills while at the same time 'depriving them of the credit which the possession of property in land confers on all other classes of men' (Campbell 1991: 110). As Campbell goes on to point out, the law of entail's restrictions 'tend very strongly to prevent improvements'.

The passing of the Rosebery Act (Entail Relief (Scotland) Act, 28 July 1836) and the Rutherfurd Act (Act for the Amendment of the Law of Entail in Scotland, 14 August 1848) finally allowed the heirs of entailed estates to disentail their land, thereby permitting them to raise credit against the capital value of their property (Duff 1848: 160–9; 178–204). In effect, these laws allowed heirs and successors to mortgage their estates to raise the funds necessary for improvements (Campbell 1991: 110).

Once the restrictions were removed, the development of Kerry of Kilfinan's agricultural sector gained momentum. The appearance of combined farms under single tenants, that can be traced to around this period, allowed improvements in husbandry and field drainage to be carried out on a relatively large – and, one must contend – realistic scale.

This had a twofold effect: first, it raised the agricultural sector above its previous subsistence base, which; second, facilitated the release of labour from the agricultural sector. The necessary conditions for economic development had been met, and Kerry of Kilfinan could, for the first time, join the Scottish Lowland mainstream.

What happened in Kerry during the mid-19th century was typical of much of the Highland experience. What was different, however, was that Kerry of Kilfinan did not experience the depopulation that was typical of much of the Highlands. Indeed, quite the reverse was true, as throughout this period Kerry of

Kilfinan's population continued to increase at a fairly rapid rate (Mitchison 1981).

Much of the explanation for this rests with Kerry's favourable location on the Clyde coast. Some Highland landowners, such as the Sutherlands, tried to encourage their dispossessed tenants into fishing and away from their ancient attachment to the land by moving them to the new purpose-built villages of Port Gower, Helmsdale and Ullapool. However, over much of the Highlands, fishing was an alien way of life, and one of which very few Highlanders had experience (Richards 1982). The residents of Kerry of Kilfinan, however, were no strangers to herring fishing, and although it was initially used merely as a supplementary means of income, it can be argued that the transition to fishing as a primary occupation would not have been one that was too difficult for many of them to make. A further attraction of fishing to many of the people of Kerry would have been the existence of a large market for the catch in the industrial towns along the Clyde. In at least this respect, the coincidence of agricultural improvement in Kerry with the arrival of the steamers was fortunate (Gray 1978).

A further happy coincidence for the inhabitants of Kerry was the establishment of the gunpowder mill during the 1840s. While fishing could be a fairly remunerative occupation that could soak up a proportion of those cast off the land, it could not sustain the lives of unlimited numbers. Those who had neither the aptitude nor the opportunity for the life of a fishermen were now presented with the alternative of industrial employment. Apart from the slate quarry at Easdale, which employed a large number of labourers, there were very few Highland parishes that had the same opportunities for industrial employment.

The arrival of the steamers not only acted as a conduit for labour and capital to leave the parish, they also brought people and capital into the parish. The Victorian love of travel is almost legendary, and the technological advances of the age brought hitherto remote areas into the reach of many. The Victorian era can, with some justification, be described as the first age of tourism.

Kerry's beautiful location on the third of Cowal's peninsulas and easy access from the industrial towns of Lowland Scotland, proved too great to resist. The unspoiled beauty of the Kyles of Bute and the ease with which the steamers could dock and passengers alight proved to be Kerry's greatest fortune.

While Kerry catered for the lower middle-class day trippers from the towns of industrial Clydeside, the real bonanza was the arrival of the wealthy upper-middle-classes who could afford to purchase land and build villas. The existing landowners, especially Scoular of Innins and Malcolm of Poltalloch, saw the popularity of similar locations at Kirn and Dunoon as summer residences of the wealthy, and grasped the opportunity to cash in on this new source of income (ABDA Register of Sasines). The marginal land on Kerry's Kyles of Bute shore was parcelled up and feud off, leading to the creation of two new villages: Tighnabruaich and Auchenlochan.

The arrival of the wealthy residents of Tighnabruaich created a demand for many new services. The houses had to be built and maintained by craftsmen and labourers, many of whom had to be brought into the area, and shops had to be opened and supplied to meet the expanding community's growing demands.

In many respects, Kerry of Kilfinan was a success story. The general experience of the Highlands was one of poverty and depopulation. This obviously did not happen in Kerry, which became a microcosm of Scottish economic development. Agricultural improvement, which many if not most economic theories believe to be an essential ingredient for successful economic development, facilitated surplus production and released labour. This labour was then used in all sectors of the economy: fishing, industry and, especially after 1850, in the service sector and construction.

However, not only was Kerry able to sustain its population, it was actually able to increase it. In effect, it became a magnet for immigrants and internal migrants (NRH Census 1841–71). Indeed, Anderson and Morse claim that the parish of Kilfinan as a whole not only sustained a natural population increase of more than 15%, but that it was also an area of net inward migration between 1861 and 1871. According to their calculations, in the Highlands as a region, Kilfinan was unique in this respect (Anderson and Morse 1990). Furthermore, the evidence presented thus far shows quite clearly that while Kerry was expanding the rest of the parish was actually in decline. We can state, therefore, that Kerry accounted for all of the expansion in the parish.

One area where Kerry does not seem to have had an experience any different from the Highland norm, however, is that concerning the poor. Despite Kerry's increasing wealth during the latter part of our period, there does not appear to be any relaxation in the application of the Poor Law. The impotent poor were still expected to rely, in the first instance, on the charity of family and friends for their relief.

However, it is true that following the Abbey parish decision in 1821, Kirk Sessions were severely restricted in the latitude they were allowed in determining who constituted the deserving poor. This situation was formalised by the 1844 Poor Law that standardised the definitions for the entire country (Mitchison 1988). The fact that Kerry was experiencing a rapid expansion in both population and employment opportunities throughout the period would suggest unemployment in the area was not a serious problem.

In 1790, it was clear that Kerry was firmly in the Highlands, suffering from the problems that were common throughout that region. The parish produced very little, if any, surplus and its inhabitants were almost entirely dependent on subsistence agriculture. Before the advent of the steamers, the area was remote and almost inaccessible to all but the most determined traveller or sailor. These factors mitigated against the development of any alternative economic sectors.

By 1870, however, that picture had changed dramatically. The arrival of the steamer opened Kerry up to the wider world. The agricultural improvements that were made possible by the Rosebery and Rutherford acts made it possible for the parish to start down the path to modern economic development. The steamers gave Loch Fyne herring access to a larger market and, consequently, provided more job opportunities in that industry.

The steamer also brought the saltpetre used in the manufacture of gunpowder from South America and then carried the finished gunpowder to its market, often as far away as New Zealand. The growth of Tighnabruaich and Auchenlochan were also dependent on the steamer, which brought the tourists, new residents and all their supplies.

While in 1790, Kerry was an economic backwater with links only to neighbouring parishes, and where the only conceivable future was one of decline, by 1870 it was firmly in the orbit of the expanding industrial Lowlands, with both national and international trading links. By this later date, it would be fair to say that Kerry of Kilfinan was 'in, but not of, the Highlands', for to survive and thrive, Kerry had to swim against the stream, and that, one may conclude, is precisely what it did.

References

Unpublished sources

ABDA (Argyll and Bute District Archives)
Abbreviated Register of Sasines – Argyll, Series 1-10
CO5/1/1 – Minutes of the Commissioners of Supply, Bute
CO6/1/1/1 – Minutes of the Commissioners of Supply, Argyll
CO6/1/11/1 – Minute Book of the General Court of Lieutenancy
CO6/1/22/4 – Abstract of the Regulations of Police
CO6/1/22/5 – Register of Voters for Argyllshire
CO6/1/8/19 – Register of Police Defaulters
CO6/1/8/4 – Police Committee of the County of Argyll
CO6/2/2 – Cowal Road Assessment 1844–55 and Minute of the Cowal
    Road Trustees
CO6/2/2/1 – Minutes of the District Meeting of Cowal
CO6/5/172/1 – Logbook of Poltalloch Madras School
CO6/5/32/1 – Minutes of Meeting of Kilfinan School Board
CO6/7/21 – Minute Book of Kilfinan Parochial Board
DR4/3/71 – The Colville Papers
Ferries in Kilfinan
Valuation Rolls 1802, 1858-9, 1863-4, 1869-70, 1874-5
SRO (Scottish Record Office)
AF26 – Loch Fyne Fisheries Records
AF37 – Correspondence Regarding Illegal Trawling in Loch Fyne
AF7/113 – Register of Fishing Boats at Rothesay
CH2/880 – Minutes of Kilfinan Kirk Session
GD9 – Inventory of the British Fishery Society Papers
HR672/1 – Kilfinan Heritors' Minute Book
SC54 – Inveraray Sheriff Court Records
NRH (New Register House)
Census of the Parish of Kilfinan 1841-71

Published sources

Act for Repairing Highways and Bridges, *Acta Parliamentorum Caroli II* (1669)

Anderson, M. and Morse, D. J. (1990), 'The people', in W. H. Fraser and R. J. Morris (eds), *People and Society in Scotland*, vol. II, Edinburgh

Argyll and Bute District Council (1988), *Buildings of Architectural and Historical Interest: Statutory and Descriptive Lists*, Lochgilphead

Argyll roads act' (1775)

Burke's Landed Gentry (1886), London

Campbell, R. H. (1991), *Owners and Occupiers*, Aberdeen

Church of Scotland (1963), *Tighnabruaich Parish Church*, Tighnabruaich

Crocker, G. (undated), *Gunpowder Mills Gazetteer: Black Powder Manufacturing Sites in the British Isles*, London

Dawson, J. H. (1853), *An Abridged Statistical History of Scotland*, Edinburgh

Dawson, J. H. (1862), *The Abridged Statistical History of the Scottish Counties*, Edinburgh

Duff, A. (1848), *A Treatise on the Deed of Entail*, Edinburgh: Bell and Bradfute, pp. 160–9; 178-204

Dundee Courier and Argus 7 and 9 December 1863; 12 March 1870

Dundee, Perth and Cupar Advertiser 28 August 1846

Ewing, Rev. W. D. D. (ed.) (1914), *Annals of the Free Church of Scotland 1843–1900*, Edinburgh

Gershenkron, A. (1962), 'Economic backwardness in historical perspective' in B. Hoselitz (ed.), *The Progress of Underdeveloped Countries*, Chicago.

Glasgow Herald 1855-7, 1870

Gray, M. (1978), *The Fishing Industries of Scotland 1790–1914: A Study in Regional Adaptation*, Oxford

Groome, F. H. (ed.) (1885), *Ordnance Gazetteer of Scotland*, vol. VI, Edinburgh

Groome, F. H. (ed.) (1894), *Ordnance Gazetteer of Scotland*, vol. VI, 2nd ed., Edinburgh

Lamont, Sir N. (1914), *An Inventory of Lamont Papers, 1231–1897*, Edinburgh

Lawson, J. P. (1842), *The Descriptive Atlas of Scotland*, Edinburgh

Levitt, I. and Smout, T. C. (1979), *The State of the Scottish Working Class in 1843*, Edinburgh

Lumsden and Sons (1839), *Lumsden's Steam Boat Companion to the Western Isles and Highlands of Scotland*, Glasgow

Macdonald, G. M. (1961), *The Third Statistical Account of Scotland: The County of Argyll*, Glasgow

Macfarlane, Rev. A. (1793), 'The Parish of Kilfinan', *The Statistical Account*, Edinburgh

Mackenzie, A. M. (1941), *Scotland in Modern Times, 1720–1939*, London

McConnell, K. J. (1984), 'The story of Kames/Millhouse gunpowder works', in H. F. Torbet (ed.), *Kilfinan: Walks, History and Reminiscences*, Tighnabruaich

McConnell, K. J. (1987), 'The people of the powder mill', *Newsletter of the Glasgow and West of Scotland Family History Society*, 24 February

McKechnie, H. (1938), *The Lamont Clan, 1235–1935*, Edinburgh

Mitchison, R. (1981), 'The Highland clearances', *Scottish Economic and Social History* 1 (1): 4–24

Mitchison, R. (1988), 'The Poor Law', in T. M. Devine and R. Mitchison (eds), *People and Society in Scotland*, vol.I, Edinburgh

Mowat, I. R. M. (1981), *Easter Ross 1750–1850: The Double Frontier*, Edinburgh

North British Daily Mail 24 September 1854

O'Dell, C. and Walton, K. (eds) (1962), *The Highlands and Islands of Scotland*, London

Parry, M. L. and Slater, T. R. (eds) (1980), *The Making of the Scottish Countryside*, London

Richards, E. (1982), *A History of the Highland Clearances*, vol. I, London

Rostow, W. W. (1959), 'The stages of economic growth', The Economic History Review 12 (1): 1-16

Shaw, F. E. (undated), 'The changing geography of Kilfinan parish', University of Newcastle.

Smith, J. (1813), *General View of the Agriculture of the County of Argyll*, London

Smout, T. C. (1969), *A History of the Scottish People, 1560–1830*, London

Smout, T. C. (1986), *A History of the Scottish People, 1830–1950*, London

Smout, T. C. and Wood, S. (1990), *Scottish Voices: 1745–1950*, London

Stark, Rev. J. (1843), 'The Parish of Kilfinan', *The Second Statistical Account*, Edinburgh

The Argyll Road Act (1800)
The Argyllshire Road Act, 56 Geo III c.70
The Argyllshire Road Act, 6-7 Victoria SESS (1843)
The Argyllshire Roads Act, 27 and 28 Victoria Cap. Ccvi.
Wilson, J. M. (1866), *The Imperial Gazetteer of Scotland: Or Dictionary of Scottish Topography*, Edinburgh